This Journal Belongs To: ____________________

35559669R00058

Made in the USA
San Bernardino, CA
11 May 2019